A Kid's Guide to Drawing™

How to Draw Cartoon Insects

Curt Visca and Kelley Visca

The Rosen Publishing Group's
PowerKids Press™
New York

Dedicated to our daughters, Kaytlin and Chloe, who enjoy exploring the world of insects in our yard

Published in 2003 by The Rosen Publishing Group, Inc.
29 East 21st Street, New York, NY 10010

First Edition

Editor: Natashya Wilson
Book Design: Kim Sonsky
Layout: Emily Muschinske

Illustration Credits: All illustrations © Curt Visca.
Photo Credits: cover photo (ladybug) © Animals Animals/Robert Maier; cover photo and title page (hand) © Arlan Dean; pp. 6, 16, 18 © Animals Animals/Patti Murray; p. 8 © Animals Animals/Robert Maier; p. 10 © Animals Animals/Stephen Dalton; p 12 © Animals Animals/Robert Lubeck; p.14 © Animals Animals/Breck P. Kent; p. 20 © Animals Animals/LSF/OSF.

Visca, Curt
How to draw cartoon insects / Curt Visca and Kelley Visca.
p. cm. — (A kid's guide to drawing)
Includes index.
Summary: This book provides information about various types of insects and step-by-step instructions for drawing them.
ISBN 0-8239-6157-5
1. Insects—Caricatures and cartoons—Juvenile literature 2. Cartooning—Technique—Juvenile literature
[1. Insects in art   2. Cartooning—Technique   3. Drawing—Technique] I. Visca, Kelley   II. Title   III. Series
NC1764.8.I57 V57 2001 2001-003901
741.2—dc21

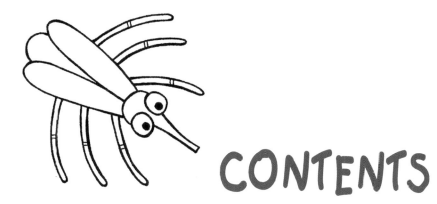

CONTENTS

Cartoon Insects

Did you know that there are more than one million different **species**, or kinds, of insects? All insects have **exoskeletons**, which means their skeletons are on the outsides of their bodies. They also have three main body parts, called the head, the **thorax**, and the **abdomen**. Insects have **compound eyes**, three pairs of **jointed legs**, and a pair of **antennae**. Most insects hatch from eggs and have wings. They undergo **metamorphosis**, which means insects' bodies change from eggs to adults in several stages. Insects live in every **habitat** except for the ocean.

In this book, you will learn some fascinating facts about eight different insects and how to draw a cartoon of each one.

As you are drawing cartoon insects, you are only going to include the basic lines and shapes, keeping your drawings simple. Cartoons are not meant to look just like real life. They show their subjects in different, often funny, ways. As you draw, you may notice that your cartoons don't look exactly like the ones on the pages. That's okay! Everyone draws with his or her own special style.

You will need the following supplies to draw cartoon insects:

- Paper
- A sharp pencil or a felt-tipped marker
- An eraser
- Colored pencils or crayons to add color

Draw your cartoons at a desk, a table, or another quiet place with a lot of light and all of your supplies nearby. Read the directions under the drawings as you add each part of the insect. The drawing shapes and terms are explained in the Terms for Drawing Cartoons list on page 22.

Remember to work slowly, to do your best, and to try to practice drawing your cartoons often. Before long you'll be a terrific cartoonist.

Don't let anything "bug" you as you get ready to draw cartoon insects!

The Ant

Ants live in
colonies that range
in size from a few
ants to millions of
ants. There are
about 20,000
species of ants! Ants'
bodies are usually
black, brown, or
red. They can be
from $\frac{1}{25}$ of an inch

(.1 cm) to 1 inch (2.5 cm) long. Ants' antennae are
bent, which makes them different from other insects'
antennae. The antennae help ants "talk" through smell,
taste, and touch.

All ants have special jobs. Queen ants are the
largest in a colony. They lay the eggs. Colonies can
have one queen or many queens. The male ants **mate**
with the queen ants and die soon afterward. The
female worker ants collect food, raise the young ants,
defend the colony, and dig tunnels. Ants can lift things
that are 50 times their weight!

1

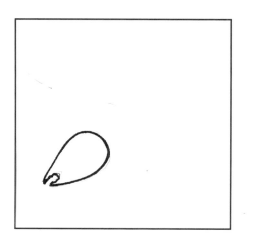

Begin by drawing a long curved line for the head and small zigzag lines for the jaws.

2

Draw two ovals and one small dot inside each oval for the eyes. Real insects have compound eyes, but we'll make simpler eyes for our cartoon insects.

3

Fantastic! Make a rounded square for the ant's thorax.

4

Make a lightbulb shape for the abdomen of the ant.

5

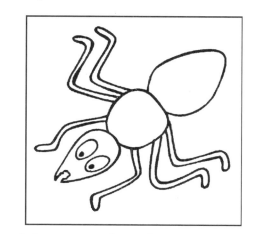

Splendid! Draw six legs, three on each side of the thorax, using long, curved zigzag lines.

6

Add detail to complete your cartoon by making the bent antennae, some dots and curved lines on the body, and a curved wiggly line for food in the ant's mouth.

7

The Ladybug

Ladybugs have rounded bodies and shiny red or orange wings with black spots. They can have from two to fifteen spots, depending on the species. There are nearly 5,000 species of ladybugs. Their bright color warns birds and other **predators** not to eat the ladybugs, because they taste bitter. Ladybugs are a big help to gardeners and to fruit farmers. Ladybugs' favorite foods are tiny insects called **aphids**, which are very harmful to plants. One ladybug can eat 5,000 aphids during its lifetime! In the winter, ladybugs **hibernate** under fallen leaves. The leaves protect the ladybugs from cold weather.

1

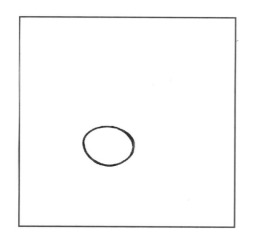

Start by drawing an oval for the head.

2

Draw two ovals inside the first oval. Add a dot inside each oval.

3

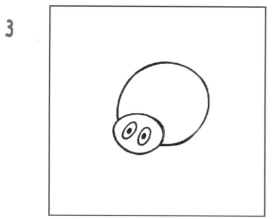

Sensational! For the body, draw a long curved line connected to the head.

4

Make six legs using short curved lines. End each leg with an oval for a foot.

5

Incredible! Draw the antennae and a small mouth. Add five shaded ovals on the body.

6

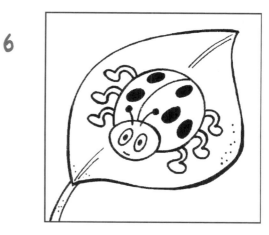

Draw a leaf using two curved lines. Add two short curved lines for the stem. Add dots and lines for detail.

The Honeybee

Honeybees are helpful to people. They make honey that we can eat and beeswax that we use to make candles. A honeybee lives in a **hive** with 40,000 to 60,000 other honeybees. Honeybees are called social insects, because they live and work together. Each hive has

one queen honeybee. She can lay up to 1,500 eggs a day. Worker honeybees gather **nectar** and **pollen** from plants. The honeybees eat the nectar and use the pollen to make honey. The worker honeybees build **honeycombs** from beeswax that their bodies make. They also guard the hive. Honeybees will sting when they feel threatened. A honeybee can sting only once. When its stinger breaks off, the honeybee dies.

1

Begin by drawing two ovals for the eyes. Add a small dot inside each oval.

2

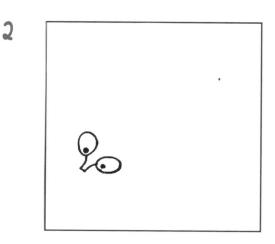

Draw two curved lines and a small line connecting them for the mouthpart.

3

I'm proud of you! Draw a curved line for the back of the head.

4

Draw two long curved lines for the wings.

5

Awesome! Draw a curved line for the body and an upside-down letter *V* for the stinger.

6

Add antennae, straight lines on the wings, stripes on the body, and action lines. Draw a flower for the honeybee.

The Dragonfly

Dragonflies have long, thin bodies and two sets of **transparent** wings. Their wingspans measure from 2 to 8 inches (5–10 cm) long, depending on the species. Their bodies are usually green, blue, or red. Dragonflies eat mosquitoes and other insects. They catch these insects in the air with their legs. When a dragonfly lays eggs, it drops them into the water or onto plants near water. When the young dragonflies, or **nymphs,** hatch, they have gills and can breathe underwater. They live underwater for one to five years. After a nymph **molts** ten or more times and is fully grown, it climbs out of the water, molts once more, and flies away. Dragonflies can fly up to 60 miles per hour (97 km/h)!

1

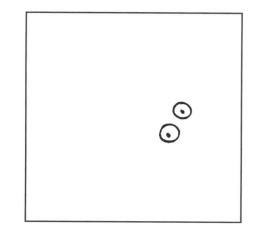

Start by drawing two circles. Add one dot inside each circle.

2

Draw two curved lines for the head.

3

Wonderful! For the thorax, make a curved line from the top of the head and a short straight line from the bottom.

4

Draw a long oval shape for the first wing and a curved line for the second wing. Add two more curved lines for the other wings.

5

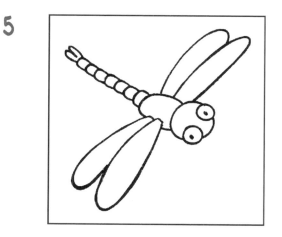

Wow! Draw seven rounded squares for the abdomen. At the end, draw two curved lines to complete the body.

6

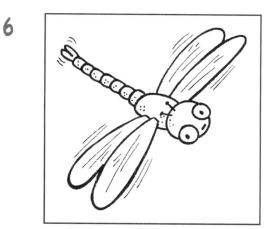

Draw a mouth, antennae, straight lines on the wings, dots on the body, and action lines. You did it!

13

The Cricket

Crickets can be heard chirping when the weather is warm. Male crickets make the chirping sounds by rubbing their front wings together. The chirping sounds help crickets find

one another. In the winter, crickets stop chirping because they are too cold to move. Crickets cannot use their wings to fly. Instead they jump by using their strong legs. Crickets hear with their front legs! Their legs have hearing organs that work like human ears. Crickets live in fields, in meadows, and sometimes in people's homes. They are **nocturnal**, which means they are active at night. They eat plants and dead insects, including other crickets!

1

Start by drawing two ovals for the eyes. Make a small dot inside each oval.

2

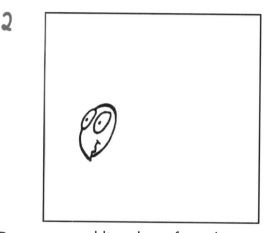

Draw a curved line down from the eye on the left and add a wiggly line and a small line for the mouth. Make a curved line for the rest of the head.

3

Nice Job! Draw a wide, backward letter L for the front leg. Add a wide letter Z for the middle leg. Make an oval attached to another wide letter L for the back leg.

4

Draw curved lines for the body and the wing.

5

Beautiful! Draw one wide, backward letter L for the second front leg. Add a wide letter L for the second middle leg. Make a wide, short letter L for the second back leg.

6

Add the antennae, some lines and dots on the body, and action lines. Make curved lines and dots for the ground.

The Firefly

A firefly is also called a lightning bug. On a warm night in the eastern United States, you can see fireflies' flashing yellow lights. A firefly uses its light to get the attention of other fireflies. The flashes attract mates and warn predators to stay away. Only the very end of a firefly's abdomen lights up. Fireflies' bodies are dark brown or black with yellow and red marks.

After firefly eggs hatch, the newborn **larvae** also give off light. Firefly larvae are **carnivores**. They eat snails, worms, and other insects' larvae. It takes firefly larvae about two years to grow into adult fireflies. Adult fireflies live only from 5 to 30 days. They eat mostly pollen and nectar, but some don't eat anything at all!

1

To begin your cartoon, draw two ovals and a small dot inside each oval for the eyes.

2

Draw a wide curved line and a small curved line for the head.

3

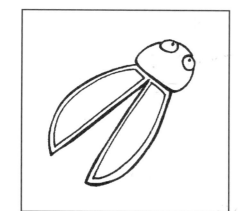

Super work! Draw a curved line and a straight line for each wing. Draw the same types of lines on the insides of the wings.

4

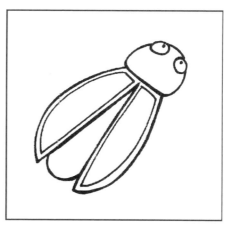

Draw a curved line for the body.

5

Great! For the two front legs, draw zigzag lines to form three parts. Make crooked rectangles for the middle and the back legs. Add small lines in the joints of each leg.

6

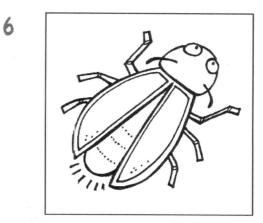

Add the antennae, the dots on the wings and body, and the straight lines at the back for your firefly's light.

17

The Walkingstick

Walkingsticks got their name because they look like slow-moving sticks. They are brown or green in color and have long, thin bodies. They are the longest insects in the United States and can grow to be up to 7 inches (17.5 cm) long! Unlike most insects, walkingsticks usually don't have wings. Their sticklike bodies blend in with the branches of the trees and the bushes on which they live. This **camouflage** hides walkingsticks from predators, such as birds. The eggs of the walkingstick are also camouflaged. They have hard shells and look like seeds. After a few months, the eggs hatch. The walkingstick nymphs, or babies, look a lot like the adults. Both the nymphs and the adults are **herbivores**, which means they eat only plants.

1

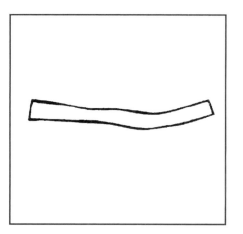

Start by drawing a long crooked rectangle for the body.

2

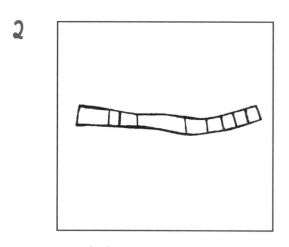

Draw straight lines on the body to show segments. A walkingstick's body segments help it look like a stick.

3

Super job! Draw and connect two zigzag lines for the first front leg, and repeat this with the second front leg. Add two short straight lines in each bend in the legs for joints.

4

Draw and connect two pairs of zigzag lines for the middle legs. Add two short straight lines in each bend in the leg for joints.

5

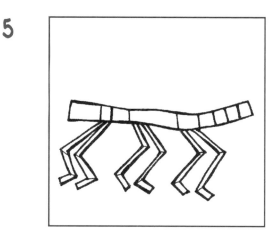

You did it! Repeat the same process to make the third pair of legs.

6

Draw antennae, dots on the body, two dots for eyes, and straight lines for a mouth. Add a tree branch.

The Mosquito

The mosquito is an insect that can annoy you when it bites. Only female mosquitoes bite! The female finds her victims by using sight and smell, and by sensing body heat. Her saliva keeps her victim's blood flowing through her mouthpart. The mouthpart, called a **proboscis**, looks like a long straw. The saliva makes the itchy bump called a mosquito bite. Male mosquitoes drink only plant nectar and water through their proboscises. Females need blood to help their eggs grow. They lay their eggs in water. One female can lay up to 3,000 eggs during her lifetime. Mosquitoes' wings beat about 1,000 times a second, making a buzzing sound. Females use this sound to find mates. Mosquitoes live in all habitats, even in the cold Arctic.

1

Begin by drawing two ovals with small dots inside. These are the eyes.

2

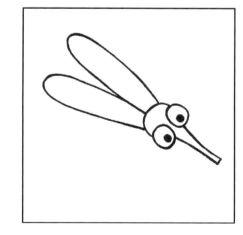

For the head, draw a curved line behind the eyes. Draw two long lines with a short line connecting them for the proboscis.

3

Outstanding work! Draw two long curved lines for the wings.

4

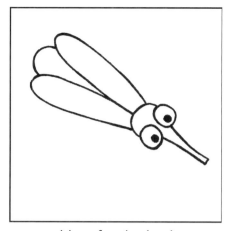

Draw a curved line for the body.

5

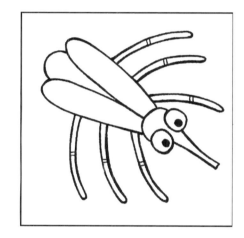

Excellent! For the legs, draw six long, skinny curved lines. Add two short lines inside of each leg for joints.

6

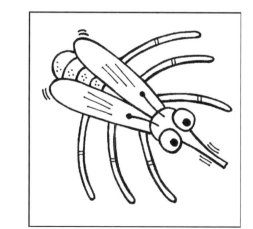

Draw the antennae. Make lines and dots on the wings and the body. Add action lines.

Terms for Drawing Cartoons

Here are some of the words and shapes that you need to know to draw cartoon insects:

𝆑	Action lines
O	Circle
▱	Crooked rectangle
⌒	Curved line
∴∴	Dots
L	Letter *L*
V	Letter *V*
Z	Letter *Z*
◠	Lightbulb shape
O	Oval
▢	Rounded square
●	Shaded oval
—	Straight line
≈	Wiggly lines
Ϻ	Zigzag lines

Glossary

abdomen (AB-duh-min) The third body section of an insect.

antennae (an-TEH-nee) A pair of thin feelers on an animal's head that help it to touch, feel, and smell.

aphids (AY-fids) Tiny insects that destroy plants by eating them.

camouflage (KA-muh-flaj) A pattern or a shape that matches an animal's background, helping it hide.

carnivores (KAR-nih-vorz) Animals that eat meat.

colonies (KAH-luh-neez) Groups of people or insects living together.

compound eyes (KOM-pownd EYZ) Eyes made up of many eyes together, which help an animal see many things at once.

exoskeletons (ek-soh-SKEH-leh-tinz) Hardened surfaces on the outsides of animals' bodies that support and protect the soft insides.

habitat (HA-bih-tat) The area where an animal or a plant naturally lives.

herbivores (ER-bih-vorz) Animals that eat only plants.

hibernate (HY-bur-nayt) To spend the winter sleeping or resting.

hive (HYV) A structure in which honeybees live.

honeycombs (HUH-nee-kohmz) Wax nets built in hives by honeybees to store honey.

jointed legs (JOYNT-id LEHGZ) Legs that can bend in one or more places.

larvae (LAR-vee) Newborn insects, hatched from eggs, that look like worms.

mate (MAYT) When a male and female join together to make babies.

metamorphosis (meh-tuh-MOR-fuh-sis) A change in appearance.

molts (MOHLTS) Sheds hair, feathers, or an outer covering.

nectar (NEK-tur) A sweet liquid found in flowers.

nocturnal (nok-TER-nul) Active during the night.

nymphs (NIMFS) Insects that are not fully grown.

pollen (PAH-lin) A powder made by the male part of flowers.

predators (PREH-duh-terz) Animals that hunt other animals for food.

proboscis (pruh-BAH-sis) A strawlike mouth through which an insect drinks its food.

species (SPEE-sheez) Animals grouped by things they have in common.

thorax (THOR-aks) The middle body section of an insect.

transparent (tranz-PAYR-ent) Able to be seen through.

Index

Web Sites

To learn more about insects, check out these Web sites:

www.bugline.com/kids.html
www.uky.edu/Ag/Entomology/ythfacts/entyouth.htm